# My 3 Lives:
## Public, Private, and Secret

Marcy Schaaf

We all have different sides of ourselves that we show to the world. Some parts we share with everyone, some only with the people closest to us, and others we keep just for ourselves.
This book will take you on a journey to discover the three lives we all live: our public life, our private life, and our secret life. You'll learn why it's okay to show different sides to different people and why some things are meant to be kept special and private.
By the end of this story, you'll understand that these three lives help make us who we are — and it's the balance of all three that lets us truly embrace our identity.
Let's explore these three lives together!

We all have 3 lives, did
you know?
Public, private, and secret
— here we go!

# Your public life is what people see.
## The side you show to society.

In public, we try to look smart and neat.
We dress in clothes that make us feel complete.

But what you wear or say may not be real.
It's how you want the world to feel.

Your public life is just for show.
It's what you want people to know.

Friends at school, teachers, and teams.
See your public side, full of dreams.

Your private life is at home, out of sight,
With family, where things feel right.

At home, people know the real
you.
Like smelly feet or favorite shoes!

You might keep secrets from
public view.
Only family and close friends
know what's true.

Even though they
see your private
side.
Your secret life is
still inside.

The secret life is deep
and hidden.
Full of things that
feel forbidden.

Your secret hopes and fears stay safe.
Locked away in a special place.

Some secrets are big,
some are small.
But everyone has
them, after all.

It's hard to let someone see this part.
Because it's the most guarded place in your heart.

If someone knows your secret
life too.
It means you really trust
them through and through.

When you know someone's 3
lives well.
That's a forever bond, can
you tell?

Public life is what you show.
Private life is what you know.

Secret life is the part that hides.
Deep within your thoughts
inside.

Most people stay in the public view.
Few will ever know the real, true you.

But when someone's in all
3 parts.
They become a piece of
your heart.

Remember, when meeting
someone new.
You're meeting their public life,
it's true.

Nobody is who they first appear.
Because their private life stays near.

And their secret life stays
hidden away.
Unless they trust you
someday.

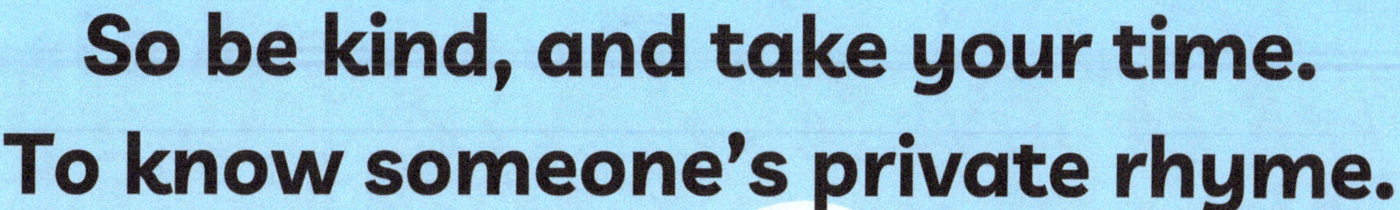

So be kind, and take your time.
To know someone's private rhyme.

The secret life is not easy to share. But knowing it shows you really care.

Everyone has 3 lives to
show.
Now it's time for you to
know!

Public, private, and secret
parts.
Make up our minds, souls,
and hearts.

It's okay to keep some things unseen.
Not everything is meant to be clean.

When you share
your secret life
with care.
It means you trust
the love you
share.

So, keep your public and
private strong.
But let your secret show
when the time's right,
along.

When all 3 lives are
open and true.
You'll know who really
cares about you!

**Public, private, secret—it's
who we are.
Together, they make us
shine like stars!**

# Join Our Book of the Month Club!

Looking for the perfect gift that keeps on giving? Join our Book of the Month Club! For just $25 a month, or $250 if you purchase a year upfront, you or your loved ones will receive a handpicked children's book every month, straight to your doorstep.

Here's how it works:
Choose from 15 different languages to receive bilingual books that make learning fun.
Enjoy monthly shipments of our exclusive books that inspire, teach, and entertain children of all ages.
Each month's book is carefully selected to provide a new adventure, valuable lesson, and a chance to explore cultures from around the world.
It's the perfect gift for birthdays, holidays, or just because! Whether you're nurturing a young reader or encouraging language learning, our Book of the Month Club is designed to bring joy to every bookshelf.

Exclusive Bonus: As part of your membership, you'll also receive a monthly podcast about our featured book delivered straight to your email! Listen in for behind-the-scenes insights, fun facts, and tips for making storytime even more magical.

Sign up today at www.Booksbyschaaf.com and start enjoying the gift of reading all year long!

# Books By Schaaf

www.BookBySchaaf.com

Find us at: